Daily
Wisdom-Light

Volume One

Sri Chinmoy

Selection from the original series of gift cards
"Heart-Wisdom-Drops", part I–III.

Madal Bal Publishing
Bartošova 40, 760 01 Zlín, Czech Republic

Copyright © 2025 Sri Chinmoy Centrum
'Soul-bird' drawings by Sri Chinmoy

All rights reserved. No part of this book may be reproduced in any form without the written permission of the publisher.

ISBN: 978-80-88324-45-4

Like the comforting words of a friend, a ray of light in the darkness, and the inspiring beauty of nature, these pearls of wisdom from Sri Chinmoy can encourage us, inspire us, guide us, and illumine us as we face each day in our life's journey.

A cheerful mind
Has always been
A perfect guide
To a healthy body.

I am happy because
I have realised the truth
That the most important
Thing in my life
Is self-improvement.

Do not be afraid of tasting
The bitterness of failure.
Be brave!
The sweetness of success
Will before long
Befriend you.

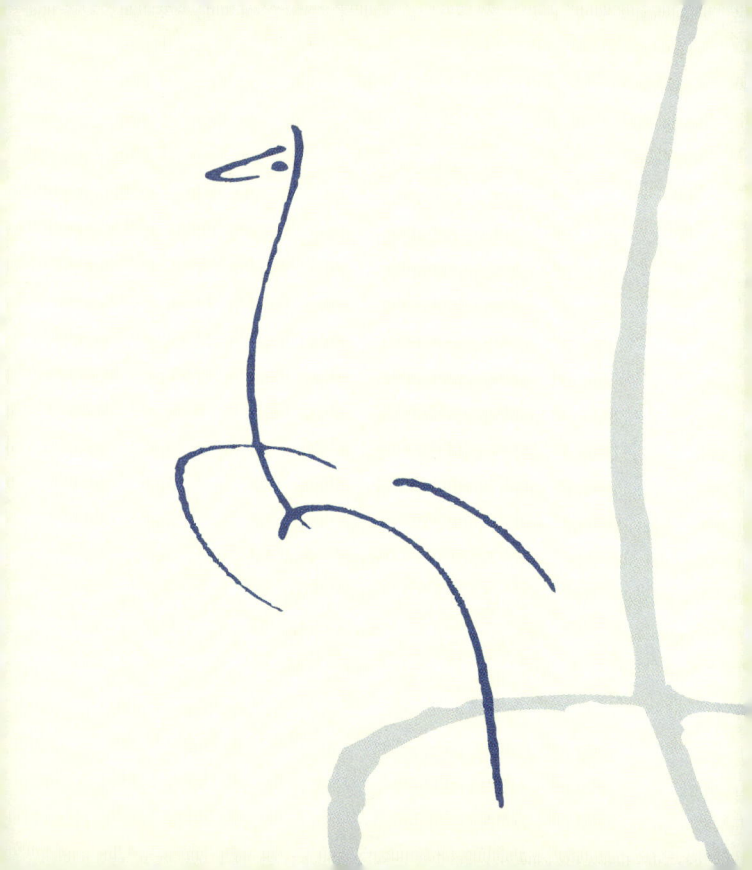

Never give up, never give up!
Even if you lose your way
A great many times,
You must realise that
   your destination
Is sleeplessly expecting
   your arrival.

Every day there is only
One thing to learn:
How to be honestly happy.

Learn the art of forgiving.
Apply it to yourself first,
Then it becomes easy
To forgive others.

The very nature of kindness
Is to spread.
If you are kind to others,
Today they will be kind to you,
And tomorrow
To somebody else.

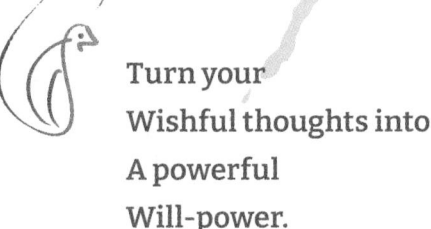
Turn your
Wishful thoughts into
A powerful
Will-power.

Wherever you go,
Carry happiness
With you.

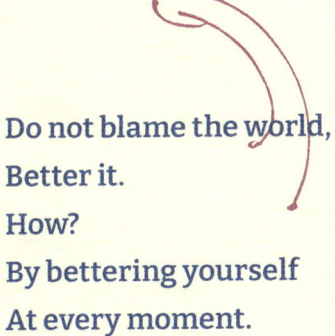

Do not blame the world,
Better it.
How?
By bettering yourself
At every moment.

A good thought
Changes everything it touches
For the better.

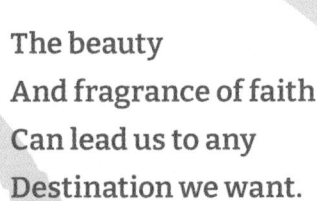

The beauty
And fragrance of faith
Can lead us to any
Destination we want.

We can change the world,
But not improve it,
If we do not have peace.

Remain cheerful,
For nothing destructive can
  pierce through
The adamantine wall of
  cheerfulness.

We can become happy
Only by seeing
The good and divine qualities
Of each and every human being.

Every moment is so sacred.
We must value it
In order to grow and glow
In our own purity-heart-garden.

A moment of
Self-giving life
Can conquer the sorrows
Of many long years.

By seeing the past
I gain nothing.
By knowing the future
I gain something.
By living in the present
I gain everything.

Do not waste
Your precious time.
Every day
Try to make it a point
To make real sense
Out of your life.

Your heart knows
How to make you happy.
Listen to your heart.

To serve

And never be tired

Is love.

Anything worth having
Is worth sharing
As well.

Be kind, be all sympathy,
For each and every human being
Is forced to fight against himself.

Always take one more step
Than you intended to.
You can, without fail, do it.
Lo, you have done it.

If you want to be
A future success,
Then do not allow
Your mind to dwell
On present defeat.

If you do the right thing,
Eventually you will inspire others
To do the right thing.

True humility
Means
Giving joy to others.

Truth is in all
But love is all.

To live in the beauty
And fragrance of the heart
Is to get younger
By the second.

I love those friends
Who treasure me
When I am right
And advise me
When I am wrong.

Do not count
Your enemies—
Your time
   Is extremely precious.
Count your friends—
And then
   Count on them.

Yesterday I was clever.
That is why
I wanted to change the world.

Today I am wise.
That is why
I am changing myself.

Love and live
And live and love
Each moment
To the fullest.

Life is a golden
Opportunity.
The sooner we realise it,
The better.

At every moment
We need cheerfulness
To surmount
All our problems.

Be not frustrated.
Once more fall in love
With your life.

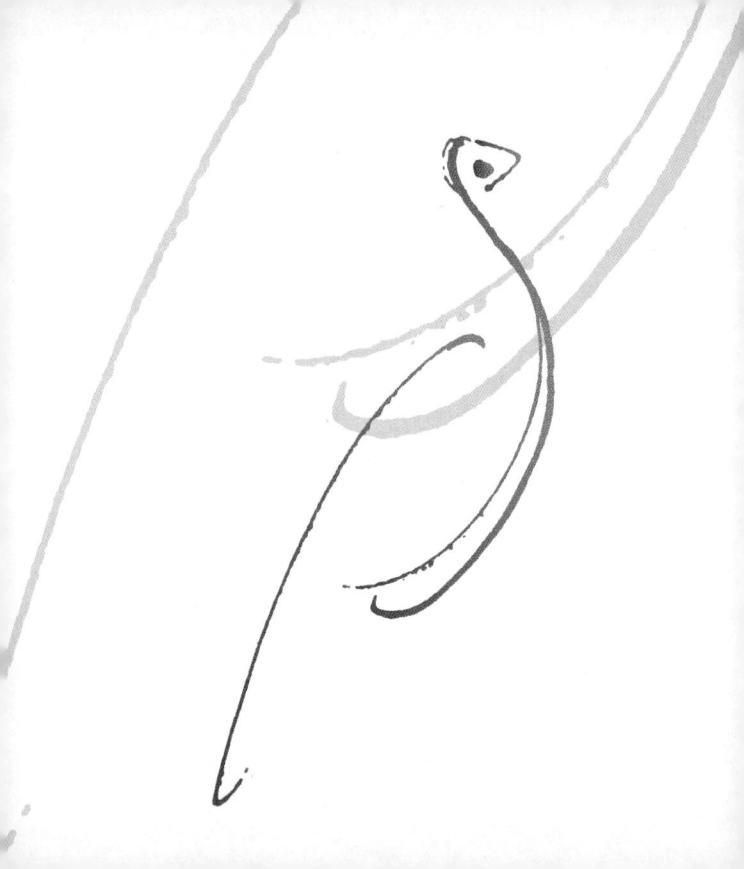

When the heart
Is happy
It embraces
The whole world.

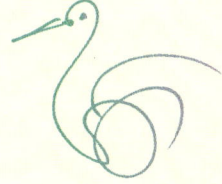

What you powerfully hold
In your thought-world
Will make you either
A street beggar
Or a great king.

I shall love
The whole world
But I shall control
Only myself.

Our real failure
Takes place
When we give up
Making further attempts.

Do not be discouraged.
Give yourself
A second chance.
You will succeed.

Daring enthusiasm
　And
Abiding cheerfulness
Can accomplish
Everything on earth
Without fail.

Trust not what you hear,
Trust not what you see,
But trust
What you feel.

The most effective
Medicine
Here on earth
Is love unconditional.

Hope
Is the strongest pillar
That protects
The entire world.

To make yourself happy,
Confess your blunders
Before you face
Any criticism.

There is only one duty
And that duty
Is to live happily.

The ordinary human mind
Is a container.
You can fill it
With good thoughts
Or bad thoughts.
It is up to you.

Character is just
What we inwardly are
And outwardly do.

**The fullness of living
Is found in
Sleepless self-giving.**

No medicine
Is as good
As hope.

We must follow,
First and foremost,
The advice that we give
To others.

We must learn
The art of appreciation.
It will be a most significant
Achievement
Of ours.

To try to measure
The power of love
Is simply ridiculous.

We must every day try
To love the essential
And not the superficial.

Do you want to understand?
Then try to love.
Do you want to love?
Then do not try to understand.

Allow failure to teach you
A supreme lesson:
Each sunset is the beginning
Of a very, very bright
And powerful sunrise.

Mine is the wisdom-light
That tells me to ask
Not for a lighter burden,
But for a stronger heart.

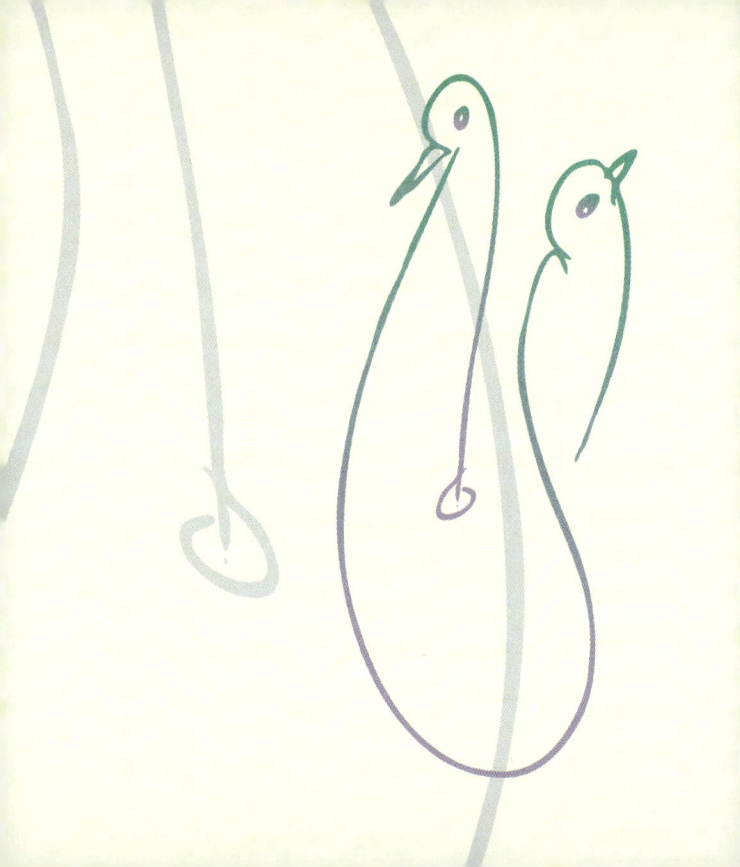

The best and most effective way
To rectify your mistakes
Is not to repeat them.

Every day
Set a new goal,
Even if you have failed
To reach your previous goals.

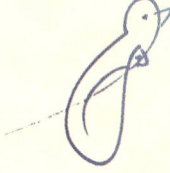

He who thrives on challenges
Can accomplish extraordinary things
   In life.

Yes I can!
I certainly can!!
I can succeed
Where nobody else
Has dared to try.

Friendship disappears when Selfishness invades.

To err is human.
But only a special person
Has the God-given divine capacity
To forgive.

To succeed in life,
What we need
Is appreciation
And not condemnation.

Be careful what you do
With your thoughts,
For each thought has and is
An atomic power.

The world needs you and me
At this very moment—
Not in the near or distant future.

When troubles
Attack you,
Just smile them away.

Any moment
Is the right moment
When we want to do
Something good.

Love
Is the only hope
Of this world.

If you wait for opportunities
To become easily available,
Then you will never be able
To succeed in life.

Do you want to change the world?
Then change yourself first.
Do you want to change yourself?
If so, remain completely silent
Inside the silence-sea.

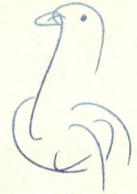

The power of love
Is extremely beautiful and fruitful.
The love of power
Is extremely dangerous
    and contagious.

The power of silence
Is the only power
That can and shall
Transform the world.

If you dare
To fail,
You are bound
To succeed.

If there is implicit faith,
The absolutely impossible
Becomes absolutely possible.

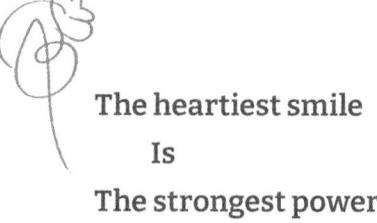

The heartiest smile
    Is
The strongest power.

Each happy life-car
Needs
An encouragement-engine.

Each human being is
    expected to be
A soulful ambassador
    of goodwill
To improve the standard
    of mankind.

Impossibility
Always bows
To humanity's
Patience-mountain.

If you can wait
With the patience of the wise,
Then there is nothing
That you will not be able to achieve
In this lifetime.

Every day you must
Prepare yourself to be
A better citizen of the world.

The love that can only forgive
But not forget,
According to me,
Is not a perfect love.

**Never allow anyone
To clip the silver wings
Of your golden dreams.**

Be true to yourself.
The world will receive
Immeasurable help from you.

ABOUT THE AUTHOR

"O my mind," says the author in one of his aphorisms, "you have talked enough. Now begin to listen. I have got a superb teacher for you. You will simply love your new teacher: heart."

And it is through the heart that he seeks to reach out to us, the readers—to inspire us to discover the light within and around ourselves, to lift us above the hardships and trials of everyday life, and to reveal our own unique role in the world.

Sri Chinmoy (1931–2007) is one of the preeminent spiritual teachers of our time. His exceptionally diverse life and teachings offer inspiration, hope and encouragement to all who seek a deeper meaning in life.

This hidden nature of our being is also reflected in his drawings of the "Soul-birds" that accompany the aphorisms in this book. May their joyful, unbound flight through the infinite inner sky remind us of our own innate freedom-light.

// srichinmoy.org

Daily Wisdom-Light
Sri Chinmoy

Selection from the original series of gift cards
"Heart-Wisdom-Drops", part I–III.
Brought to life by Madal Bal Publishing.
First edition 2025.